A
Prayer
For
The
Common Person

**The Lord's Prayer as seen through
God's Heavenly Mansion.**

John 14:2 There is plenty of room for you in my Father's
home. If that weren't so, would I have told you that I'm on
my way to get a room ready for you? (The Message)

An adaptation from the sermon series:
The Lord's Model Prayer
Presented by Reverend Stephen Crowell, M.Div.

With devotional notes and questions by:
Peggy Buelow and Lee Capodagli

1

ACKNOWLEDGEMENTS

If you were to ask any and all honest pastors, they would all agree that they have very few original thoughts. We are constantly on the hunt for new ideas, stories, illustrations and life experiences to better proclaim the Good News given to us by our Lord, Jesus. On the way to a wedding, I was asked by my organist to explain the Lord's Prayer. She, as well as the others in the church, repeated this prayer week after week. It had lost its meaning to her and she wanted to again be fully connected with what Jesus had taught.

I went home to my library and searched the shelves for books and illustrations on this prayer. The ideas for the 'House of Prayer' concept that I have used in my sermons and here in this book came from several resources, scripture and also from the Internet. More specifically a website that Parva Press developed to promote John Belham's book: "Lord, Teach Us to Pray." At that time he was the Rector of several rural parishes in England. He, in turn, also took the ideas from a fellow clergyman named Dr. J.I. Packer, who had written several articles for inclusion in different religious magazines.

I am truly grateful for Kristan, my wife, who has endured my intrusion on her time week after week during our ministry. I rely on her critical thinking and her ability to challenge my thought process. She has become an invaluable partner in all of our endeavors. I am truly grateful God put her into my life.

The Lord has also sent my way a brother in Christ that has walked with me for many years. Almost daily Craig Buelow has held my feet to the fire. He is also invaluable as we share the pulpit in our joint charge. He lends great wisdom to our ministry.

I am also grateful to those awesome churches that I serve each week. They have allowed Craig and me to experiment with different worship ideas. During the presentation of these sermons the worship team would add a portion of a room each week. Each one of us has a particular learning style. My goal is to reach everyone that comes to our churches though sound, touch and sight. I am finding that many learn through their vision. With this in mind I try to create a three dimensional environment to bring God's words to life. Also, on the power point screen I use pictures to complement the words.

I would also like to extend my thanks to Peggy Buelow and to Lee Capodagli in their work helping me to develop the weekly devotional. They spent time going over the text and researching different scriptures to bring forward questions that help each of us to dig deeper mining this prayer on deeper thought and action levels.

CONTENTS

-

PREFACE

For far too many people the Lord's Prayer is only known as part of their Sunday morning experience. Each Sunday all across this vast world of ours many find themselves repeating this prayer in unison with those sitting or standing around them. It is my experience that the majority of those repeating the prayer truly have not taken the time to fully understand those few words Jesus taught the disciples. The mystery of this prayer is that the vast majority of those who take the time to repeat this simple, yet complex prayer will find comfort in the mere act of its repetition.

This feeling of comfort should not be enough! It is through the Lord's Prayer that we can find the ultimate power to live out our daily lives with a sense of inner fulfillment. Jesus was not teaching this prayer to women and men of privilege. No, Jesus was speaking directly to the **common person** of his day. The content of this prayer deals directly with the questions and situations that we have to contend with each and every day.

In truth, this world hasn't changed. Common people still want to know where their place is within the scheme of things. Who and where is God? How do we live day to day? How am I supposed to live my life? Many of us have become accustomed to the norm of living paycheck to paycheck. Haven't we all wondered about being forgiven from our bad behaviors? When do we dare forgive others for the misdeeds that affect us?

The goal for us as we explore this awesome prayer is to break with our tradition of just reciting a ritual prayer at home or in church. We are going to take the time to truly explore the depth of this prayer. Jesus is the master of creating layers of meaning upon layers of meaning. He told stories to those around so that each time they heard the story it could have a deeper meaning. It is the same with this prayer that he taught to his disciples.

In his book, "Lord, Teach Us to Pray" Rev. Belham used everyday illustrations based on various special rooms found in a large expansive house. I intend to use some of these same rooms and their contents to guide our discussion so that we can more fully understand this prayer that Jesus gave the twelve disciples. Today, we who are modern-day disciples may continue in the footsteps of the twelve by digging deeper into this prayer or mining its depths for examples on how to live in today's complicated world.

Our mission will be to explore the Lord's Prayer like we would explore a large mansion that we had been invited to visit. It is similar to a guided tour of old and famous mansions around the country like the Vanderbilt on Long Island, Elvis' Graceland in Tennessee, and those of the rich and famous in Tinsel Town. This house of prayer will have many rooms to explore. The various rooms will match up with the different phrases found in the Lord's Prayer.

You may find, like I did, that every time I come back into a room there is so much more to explore. Since each room is so filled with many different items to view and examine, each room or phrase opens to us a different truth about God's world.

Beware; we have a tendency to want to rush around so we can check off each location. I have led many backpacking trips over the years. I find it interesting that most of the college students wanted to test themselves to see just how many miles they could complete in one day. They rushed forward at breakneck speeds. Their eyes were only focused on the next step so as not to stumble. At the end of the day when I arrived at camp, I loved to quiz them about the different wonders they saw on the trail. They would give me this blank stare – and come up with little to no answer.

They were concerned about the distance and forgot about the fact that they went to the woods to enjoy God's nature. If they had asked me what I saw, I could tell them about the little waterfalls in the streams where the trout would hide in the rocks. I could share with them about the fossils that held footprints from animals that have long been dead, or the way the light danced through the trees giving my soul an easy peaceful feeling. I normally arrived at camp some time after they did, but my soul was filled with all that I saw.

I challenge you to read through this book taking the time to let it sink into your soul. Don't be like my college students that would race through this book just to complete the goal or task of finishing an assignment. Instead, if you slow down and pace yourself, this prayer will transform your life by revealing some small nuggets of truth. You will learn that God is not distant, but wanting to impact your daily life. Our Creator has put together a plan where we find joy in deep relationships with others, ourselves and with the Trinity.

It is our goal to break down the Lord's Prayer into small manageable bites. You will explore four major components in each chapter that will guide you to a deeper understanding of each phrase of the Lord's Prayer.

> First, each chapter will start off with a tour of a particular room within the mansion.

>Next, the prayer is broken down using the room, scripture, and other illustrations to unpack the phrase.

>Then, each chapter will have a sample prayer.

>At the close of each chapter there will be a seven day devotional for deeper exploration. Each Sunday you will be given the opportunity to experiment with writing your own prayer.

We pray that through this book and the power of the Holy Spirit you will find the information and strength to direct your daily path of life. New strength will be given to you as you fight your daily battles. I believe that you will find new strategies to win the fight against evil.

Father, I come to you now asking that you will reveal yourself to those that will read this book.

Help us to reveal your words and truth so those who may be searching for your will in their lives may find the answers.

Father, I pray that your name will be lifted up as each reader finds a new respect for you.

Give each person reading this book a release from their worry about how they will live each day. You have them in the palm of your hand.

Help each person to find forgiveness as they learn to forgive those who have hurt them.

Thank you for each test so that when the Lion roars we too will be ready for battle.

Thank you for your son that came to us as a living sacrifice. Help each reader to give you all the praise you deserve. Amen

Devotional Information & Instruction

Mining for Understanding

Our mission in writing this book is to not only give you stimulating information concerning the Lord's Prayer, but to also provide a platform for you to become involved in finding answers that are pertinent to your life. This book is designed to be read slowly. This book can and should be read with the goal of one chapter per week. So then at the close of each chapter there will be a seven day devotional experience to guide you as you dig deeper into the current topic found in the chapter. Take control of your personal tour of this mansion, use your time wisely by setting aside time each day to reread those sections that align with the daily devotional. Truly use each weekly session to make the Lord's Prayer personal to you and to your needs. This prayer is for the common person.

Beware; slow down and truly explore the gift that Jesus has given us. Enter each room with care; be sure to look around so that you learn all that you can. Try this experiment that I have used in our worship services.

Look around the room you are currently in, study it well, and then close your eyes. Try to remember everything that you saw. Make a mental list. Now open your eyes. Could you remember all the various items that are found in the room?

No, even though you have been in this room thousands of times you still could not recall all of the items. This is similar to this model prayer. Every time you come back to it you begin to see more and more. Now, when you enter the room you begin to consciously remember more of what is around you. Remember, each time you return to an area something new comes to mind, something that the Holy Spirit guides you to. Allow the Spirit to give you the wisdom to seek.

Saturday – Personal Reflection

Each chapter is meant to be somewhat of a quick read. Make a commitment to set aside time each Saturday to begin your spiritual journey with reading one chapter. After your reading use the space provided to write down the different thoughts that come to mind. Then put down the book and go about your day. Allow the information to simmer just below the surface. It will begin to bubble up just like indigestion. Let this by your guide.

Sunday – Personal Prayer Experimentation

Prayer is no more than a conversation with the Triune God. As a pastor it is difficult for me to fully understand the reluctance many have with going to their Creator in prayer. Prayer is a special gift given to each and every one of us. Prayer is not only for emergencies when only God can respond, or when we have reached depths of despair and we are driven to our knees in prayer. Prayer is for those times when a parking space is needed, or with temptations that drive us insane.

Each Sunday explore different ways to communicate with the Triune God. Some conversations are with the Spirit seeking wisdom, or with Jesus seeking personal strength, or with the Father seeking forgiveness.

Monday through Friday

The daily devotions can be done individually, in a covenant group, or with a partner. We recommend that you have available a study Bible that has a concordance for word studies. You may use reputable sites on the internet to search the scripture by word or by phrase.

I have downloaded to my computer e-Sword so that I can compare different translations. Also, on the internet you may find commentaries to help explain the different passages. A word of "Caution:" not all that is on the net is truthful and helpful.

John Wesley, the founder of the Methodist movement, established four ways to test materials. Foundational to all study is scripture. Scripture can and should be used to test all points found in scripture and all other ideas. Next is tradition, this may be difficult for some outside of the traditional church. In short, what has the church believed to be true? The church has been functioning since Jesus' death. Our creator also gave us a brain to use. We are encouraged to use reason. This is where we can compare different ideas against scripture. Lastly is what has been our experience with the issue. What has God shown us to be true? Most want to start here, but this is just a test of the other three.

FOREWORD

Our world is overwhelming.

Our world is filled with mystery.

Our world causes us to be filled with anxiety. Media outlets reveal to us the terrors of war, the devastating results of floods and tsunamis, and the horrific damage fire creates in families. Commercials are designed to cause our hearts to break when we see the tearstained cheeks of homeless starving children.

What can we do?
Where can we turn?

In our despair our inner spirit calls out. On our spirit level, we find ourselves crying out to a god. Even before we have come to a point in life where we have consciously given our lives over to our Lord, our spirit knows to cry out.

I am comforted to know that, when each of us are having struggles and our lives are falling apart, God, the creator of the Universe, has prepared a plan for the world that each and every person would be able call upon the Trinity for help. Humanity has always been in a mess and we have needed a way out of our problems. Our nature and character has caused a separation from our Creator. No matter what we did in and of ourselves, we could not find a way back. Before time began, Jesus had been the answer to the problem.

Jesus, who is God the Son and part of the Trinity, humbled himself to become part of the creation story. He entered into our world as a baby. He grew into adulthood facing all of the same problems that the rest of us face. Yet, through the power of the Holy Spirit dwelling in him, he was able to be perfect. Jesus became our role model on how to live. His greatest commandments for us are to love God and to love others. It took his death on the cross to take away our misdeeds and it took his resurrection to give us a promise of eternal life with the Trinity.

Today, the Holy Spirit calls to us through our brokenness and softens our heart and soul so that we can again fall in love with Jesus. When we recognize Jesus, he leads us back to his Father. We will see in the first chapter that Jesus brings us into the very presence of God the Creator in the Grand Foyer. It is there that we are presented worthy to be called daughters and sons of the King.

The disciples had a unique experience. They lived with Jesus. In spite of this, they still had feelings of helplessness. The disciples saw Jesus' example of praying daily. They knew that it must be something special and wanted to find the same peace that Jesus had.

Here's the interesting part that I find comforting. We think that we should know how to pray instinctively. Yet, we struggle in knowing how to pray, so did the disciples. They had to ask Jesus to teach them to pray. Like us, they wanted to do it right. Jesus then took the disciples aside so that he could teach them what we now call the 'Lord's Prayer'.

The Rev. Dr. John Belham nails it with this statement from his book, "Lord, Teach Us to pray." "Jesus didn't give this model to us only to be thought of as a literary masterpiece to be admired. Nor was it to be some ritual prayer with lovely words to add beauty to our lives. It was to be a pattern for prayers that will give us power to overcome all of our worldly concerns."

It is a real prayer for real people to deal with the real world. (J. Belham)

◈❧✦❧✦❧✦

SATURDAY

◈❧✦❧✦❧✦

(place your reflections on this page)

❧ ॐ ॐ ॐ ❧

Sunday

❧ ॐ ॐ ॐ ❧

(place your prayer or prayers here)

MONDAY

Jesus would regularly to go off by himself to pray. This was not the normal activity for common everyday Jews. Soon those following Jesus asked him to teach them about prayer. This prayer was meant to be a practical prayer for common everyday folks. See Matthew 4:18-21, Mark 3:16-19, Matthew 9:9 to meet those that Jesus called.

What did they do for a living?

Jesus left the desert to begin his ministry in his hometown. It was there that he read from the scroll and declared his 'mission' for his ministry. Read Luke 4:16-22

Who do you consider to be poor?
Can you be rich and still be poor?
What about poor in spirit?

In our life, what can what can hold us captive?
Are we captives?

What did Jesus mean by giving sight to the blind?

What does being oppressed look like
and how are they set free?

The concept of Jubilee goes back to the Old Testament when all of the debts were forgiven. Cool Eh!

22

෯ᔤᲖᔤᲖᔤ৯

TUESDAY

෯ᔤᲖᔤᲖᔤ৯

On page seven, Stephen wrote that this prayer was for the common person of his day. Yesterday the lesson revealed who Jesus had chosen to be his disciples. John, Peter and some of the others were called from the sea where they were fisherman. Matthew was a tax collector. These were common everyday jobs. There were women who followed after Jesus who would also be in the common category. Read Luke 10:38-42 & John 8:1-12.

Yesterday the lesson also looked at the 'mission' of Jesus. Would you place those who are poor, captive, oppressed and blind as part of those we would call common?

What are some characteristics of being common?
Who would be called common today?

One characteristic that is important to our study is the one common thread found among the followers of Jesus which is that they all were willing to look to Jesus for the truth in the world. They saw that Jesus was authentic and had answers that would work. Are we willing today to take this radical Jesus at his word and make Jesus Lord or King of our life?

≈ଏ⃝ଉଏ⃝ଉଏ⃝୨
WEDNESDAY
≈ଏ⃝ଉଏ⃝ଉଏ⃝୨

In Matthew 9:9-13 Jesus is seen inviting Matthew the tax collector to join him. Matthew immediately got up from his tax booth and followed Jesus. Jews who became tax collectors were looked down upon by other Jews. Jewish people felt that these collectors had sold them out to the Roman government. They were also suspected of being thieves, because they would take more than what the government had assigned.

The passage continues to show that Jesus went home with Matthew. Before leaving with Jesus he threw a large party with his friends. The Bible says that these friends were other tax collectors and sinners.
How does one become sinful?

Jesus was asked why he would sit with those that he knew were sinners. What do you think of his answer in verses twelve and thirteen?

Read James 4:17 for a definition of sin. Could sin be defined, then, as one doing what they desire or choosing to follow after their own free will?

✦ℰ✦ℰ✦ℰ✦
THURSDAY
✦ℰ✦ℰ✦ℰ✦

Yesterday the lesson ended with a definition of sin. Choosing one's will over God's will is defined as sin. It is this sin then that causes a separation between the Creator and the created. Read Genesis 2:25 – 3:24 to review the story of Adam and Eve in the Garden.

Why do you think they chose to eat the forbidden fruit?

Was it the fact that they ate the fruit or was it more than that? Could it have been a battle of wills?

Has everyone sinned and turned away from God?
Read Romans 3:23

Is there a way to be saved from our sins?
Read Romans 5:8&9

What must we do then to be saved?
Read Romans 10:9-13 & Ephesians 2:4-8

What a gift to each one of us that the Triune God cared enough about us to call us to Jesus for our salvation! Read the following verses to witness the working of the Holy Spirit in our lives: John 6:44-45, 12:32, Titus 2:11-13, Philippians 2:12-13

~ɛ)ɾɛ)ɾɛ)ϑ

FRIDAY

~ɛ)ɾɛ)ɾɛ)ϑ

When Jesus declared his ministry in his hometown, he publically declared that his mission was to the poor, downtrodden, blind and those without hope. Just before his death Jesus passed that mantle on to us, his followers. Jesus had been giving those listening to him a glimpse into heaven and at who would be there. Jesus ended these stories with a description of who would be allowed in. Read Matthew 25:41-46 for a short description or read the entire chapter for the long version.

Being part of the family of God comes with some requirements. Children of God do not get a free ride to heaven. Jesus' ministry on earth was a model for our actions. After reading this text, what do you feel the Creator God has called you to do in the here and now?

Do people suffer in this world because we are only concerned about our own needs instead of looking out for others? Is this sin?

THE GRAND ENTRY

FOYER

CHAPTER ONE

Matthew 6:9 (NIV)
"Our Father in heaven"

Jesus leads the disciples and us out from the world that is filled with distress, pain, hunger, and loneliness. Jesus brings us into a new spiritual kingdom that his Father rules. Within this kingdom is the palace that is to be our new home. Jesus promised us when he left us that he would go and prepare a place for us.

Picture all of the grand palaces that you have seen in pictures. These large homes sit in the middle of fine green lawns that are perfectly manicured. The front lawn is divided by a cobblestone drive that is edged with trees and low cut shrubbery. This driveway curves around to the front entry that has a roof that extends over the drive so that visitors, guests and family will not be hampered by any inclement weather.

As we ride up the cobble path, the house is so large that we are unable to take in all of the intricate details. It is more beautiful than one could ever imagine. Extensions come out from the main house. The golden roof gives off sharp glints of light from the rays of the sun that cause the air to virtually shimmer.

Jesus, full of excitement, has to practically drag us from the carriage to the front doors. These double doors are also covered in gold. Scenes of seraphim and cherubim bringing messages to earth are deeply carved into the many panels. A slight rush of wind blows the doors open to reveal the grand foyer.

Walking into this great room you are able to see that there are many doors leading off to smaller rooms. On either side of this grand foyer there are two grand marble staircases with wrought iron railings leading both to the left and to the right up to the balcony that encircles the entire room.

In the center of this scene is God the Creator in full glory. At once your eyes are drawn into those eyes that reveal a great love for his children. Jesus is pulling each and every one of us to come closer. God, the Father, is reaching out, bidding the disciples and you to come closer.

28

Words of warmth and tenderness welcome all to their new home.

This first scene would have come as a complete surprise to the disciples. This scene is similar to the first phrase of the prayer. Our Father in heaven is how Jesus tells us to begin our prayer. Jesus is drawing us directly into the presence of his Father to have a conversation. Remember that a prayer is nothing more than a conversation with one of the Trinity.

Up until this point, an average Jewish person would have never thought that they could have gone directly in prayer to their God. If they were to pray they would have started: Father Abraham, who walked with God, take our prayers to God for us, please continually speak for us. Or maybe they would have picked Moses. Then the prayer would have sounded like: Father Moses, you had the awesome privilege to speak with God face to face. Pray for us. Just as you were able to see God face to face, please now seek his presence and let him know the trouble we are facing. They could have picked any one of their spiritual leaders and inserted their name. Instead they relied on their priest to communicate with God.

In this prayer for common people, Jesus proved himself again to be a radical in his teachings. Jesus invites us to enter into the presence of God with boldness. Just sit and think about this as we enter into God's presence. This is the God that out of nothing breathed the Universe into existence. The world was formed for us: to live in, and to explore, and to find Joy in building a relationship with the Trinity.

We are mere specs of dust in the scheme of it all; yet, the Creator invites us to come into the very presence of God the Father with all that we are concerned about. Look at it more on our terms. Imagine if someone you highly respected called for you to visit with them. Wouldn't you drop all that you were doing to come? Why? Because, we value and respect their position of authority.

You wouldn't just saunter into their home or office. I imagine you would enter with eyes wide open taking in everything that you could. This may be your only chance to visit and you want to remember it all in great detail. In fact, you may enter with fear and trembling.

How do we address God?   (Our Father)

Jesus teaches in the first line that we are to call Him "Father." God created the human race to have a close relationship with Him. Sin causes us to feel separated from our Father. Satan's mission is to keep us feeling that God is the creator who sits on a throne in the heavens, and who is unobtainable for humans in this life. Yet, God craves for us to come to him calling him "Father." He has given us an example that is easy to mirror. The example given is the relationship that most of us have with our earthly fathers.

If you are like me, I call my dad at least every other day. If I don't, he calls me to see what is wrong. We will talk for long periods of time about nothing or about deep disturbing subjects. I don't have to worry that I am bothering him or that he will reject me.

This was radical thinking for the Jewish community. They never had the ability to talk with God directly. Israelites met God through the priests at the Tabernacle or later in the Temple. They held the name of their God, Yahweh in high esteem. Often in the Old Testament when people spoke to God they did so through angels or other means of mediation. Moses spoke to Yahweh and then had to cover his face because of the glow that radiated from him. Through Jesus' death the door to heaven has been opened for us to enter.

The power of 'Our'

Look again at how the prayer opens. It uses the word 'our'. It doesn't matter who you are or your position in life. We are all invited to come to the Father. Our God is

31

seeking to have a deep and powerful relationship with each one of us. We could be a carpenter, a king, a servant, or a farmer. This is to be a common prayer for each one of us to enter God's presence.

As we are beginning to come to the Father in heaven we are to become aware that we are part of the whole body. We enter with a sense that we are bringing others with us, if only in spirit. It should move our hearts to be thinking of others instead of focusing only on our own problems. Jesus with this opening is teaching us to immediately take our focus off from self. Jesus does not give us the option to enter by saying My Father or just Dear Father.

Jesus sets the ground work for developing a community mindset. First, we are in relationship with the Trinity, God the Father, God the Son, and God the Holy Spirit. Second, we are in community with other believers. These are our sisters and brothers that together we grow deeper in our mutual experiences. Lastly, we are part of the larger creation. We have a responsibility to care for others and for this physical world on which we live.

Matthew (22:34-40) records an encounter between Jesus and a lawyer. The lawyer wanted to know which commandment of the Mosaic Law was the most important to follow. These are the words that Jesus answered with:

Love the Lord (which means king) your God with all of your heart, mind, and soul. Jesus continued to say that loving your neighbor as oneself was the second most important action one could do.

The power of "our" brings us into God's presence with a different attitude. We now come boldly not always for self, but with others on our minds. We come to seek God's will. We come to seek God's blessing. We come to lift up the needs of this world and others so that they will be blessed also by the presence of God.

The meaning of Our Father "in heaven"

The kingdom of God and the kingdom of heaven has been revealed through scripture to have two distinct meanings. Matthew in his gospel includes "in heaven" I believe because he is writing mainly to his people, the Jews. Matthew apparently feels that it is important to place God in a physical location. The Israeli nation had been looking for a messiah or a savior to free them from their physical bondage to other nations. The Old Testament shows their struggle of faith. They would follow after God for a time then they would begin to chase after other gods. Their God, Jehovah, would allow other nations to invade

Israel. Several times the people were taken off into captivity.

Jehovah had always come to their rescue. The Roman Empire was now one of those conquering nations. The streets were filled each and every day with soldiers making demands on them. This is why Jesus gave them a hope for the future when God would take over this world in a physical and political way. Jesus would call them to repentance for the kingdom of God is at hand. He was reminding them of their history and of the hope of salvation.

Jesus also spoke of the kingdom that was to come. Throughout scripture we are told that we are more than just children of God, we are heirs to the kingdom. In the small New Testament book Titus we read in chapter three that the Holy Spirit was poured out on us by Jesus, our king and our Savior. We are brought into the kingdom of God as heirs. We have a physical home with the Trinity in a time that is yet to come.

Luke mainly refers to the kingdom of God as a spiritual kingdom that is in the here and now. One could look to the seventeenth chapter of Luke. Starting with verse twenty, Jesus was being asked by the Pharisees when the kingdom of God would come. Jesus said to them that they could not tell by looking for it either here or there because the kingdom of God resides within believers.

Followers of Jesus now understand that they can reestablish their broken relationship with the Triune God in the here and now. As part of the outpouring of love within this relationship, people desire to fulfill the will of God. Jesus came to meet the needs of those who were lost, sick, broken and in need of hope. Jesus set for us the example. During the last hours on earth Jesus gave us direction to do likewise (Matthew 25). We are to become partners with God in doing God's will on earth in the present time.

Father; it is so great to be able to come to you as your child. Remember my brothers and sisters today as we look to you.

＜§℥∞ℭᎪ℥∞ℭᎪ℥Ꭹ∾

SATURDAY

＜§℥∞ℭᎪ℥∞ℭᎪ℥Ꭹ∾

(place your reflections on this page)

◈🙟◖🙟◖🙟❧

Sunday

◈🙟◖🙟◖🙟❧

(place your prayer or prayers here)

Monday

We all come to this prayer with ideas already set in our mind. Stephen is taking a bold step here in allowing us to re-imagine the Lord's Prayer juxtaposed or in view of Jesus promise to us his sisters and brothers that there is a mansion with many rooms that he is preparing for us.

How would you imagine your mansion to look?

Would Jesus include those styles that make you distinctly you?

What would you have included if you were allowed to ask?

Waterfalls?

Paisley wallpaper?

Describe the perfect mansion just for you.

Stephen mentioned that an average Jewish person of the Old Testament would have approached God in prayer through an intermediary. Now, in teaching his disciples to pray, Christ encourages us to come to, and converse with, the Father directly.

Consider how it makes you feel to enter into the very presence of God and to speak with the Creator of all that we see and don't see.

Frightened?

Excited?

Ashamed?

Do these feelings change as the subject of your conversation with the Father changes, as you come to Him with prayers of thankfulness, of praise, with requests, both personal and for others, or to ask forgiveness for sins or for guidance?

Make a list of the feelings you have for each type of prayer you pray (remember that each time you pray you may be incorporating several of these types of "mini-prayers" into your entire prayer). Try and list as many feelings for each type of prayer as you possibly can.

Does scripture back up Stephen's statement that we can enter God's presence with boldness?
Read Acts 4:29-31, Ephesians 3:11-12, Hebrews 4:16

In the Foreword, Stephen talked about those in the world being separated from God through their sinful nature. In this chapter, Stephen again writes that Satan has a mission to keep us from feeling that we can enter God's presence. Revelations 3:1-3 talks about Satan being thrown into the pit so that the nations would not be deceived, do you think that we are separated from God because we have stupid thinking?

What do you think the curtain in the Temple being torn apart during the crucifixion of Jesus means to us today? Matthew 27:51

Editor's note: The curtain in the Temple kept all eyes off from the Mercy Seat in the Holy of Holies. The High Priest was allowed to go into this sacred room only once per year to make the Sacrifice of the Atonement for the Israelite people. It was at this time the High Priest would ask the Lord God for forgiveness for all the people.

≪ঞৣঞৣঞ৶

THURSDAY

≪ঞৣঞৣঞ৶

Stephen desires that all who read this book and follow after Christ clearly know that they are the children of God and have been known before the creation of the Universe. Paul, in his letter to the Ephesians, sheds light on this topic throughout the book, but the first chapter clearly defines God's role in our lives.

Ephesians 1:4a We were chosen before the foundations of the world were laid.

Ephesians 1:4b Through Christ's death on the cross we were made to be holy and blameless. The plan from the beginning was to save us from our own stupidity.

Ephesians 1:5 God, the Triune God, the Creator of the Universe and all that we know chose us from the very beginning to be adopted into the family of God. It was Their pleasure and will.

Ephesians 1:11 Through Christ's work we have also obtained an inheritance. Verses 13 & 14 reveal that the Holy Spirit has marked us as Their own. We will receive our inheritance in Heaven as God's own people.

Let this sink into your soul. We have been marked by God to be His child since before the world was put into place. Awesome!

≪ॐ൰ॐ൰ॐ൰ॐ≫
FRIDAY
≪ॐ൰ॐ൰ॐ൰ॐ≫

Now, examine your list from Tuesday's lesson and consider each feeling you listed individually. Begin to ask yourself, "Does feeling this while I'm praying help or hinder my communication with my Father?"

If it holds you back, get rid of it! Consciously banish it from you mind before you begin to pray. If it heightens your ability to talk to the Father, if it helps you approach him in sincerity and openness, embrace it, focus on it, let it fill your mind as you wait in silence for His still, small voice to speak to you.

As you are examining your lists, physically cross out the negative or emotionally limiting things you wrote down.

When you have finished examining each item, make a new list of the enabling ones that remain, printing them in large bold type. HOW WILL THIS HELP/CHANGE MY PRAYER LIFE??? Use this as a visual reminder to help develop the mind-set you want each time you prayerfully approach "Our Father, who art in heaven…"

THE MASTERíS OFFICE

CHAPTER TWO

Matthew 6:9 (NIV)
"Hallowed be your name"

Jesus quickly wants to prove how important His Father is to us. It was important first to meet the One that created not only each and every one of us, but the entire creation, seen and unseen. It is by meeting God the Creator directly and personally that we can begin to grasp how important we are. The Trinity cared enough about us that a way was made for us to return to God.

Jesus wants us to be reminded of this commitment. It is in this side room off from the Foyer that we can begin to see the wonder and cost of that commitment. Jesus takes each of us into a room where we can offer our respect to God. Almost any office holds the articles that are important to the one who resides there.

If you were to come into my office today, you would first notice the layout of the room. I have placed the furniture in very specific areas. The desk is pulled away from the wall with a seating area in front of it. This allows for formal conversation to take place. This is where I hold official meetings. Off to the side I have another chair that I can use for more informal settings.

Behind the desk is a long counter where I keep an array of framed photos. Kristan, my wife, fills many of the frames along with my children. These photos are snapshots of important phases of our life together. Some photos are from our vacations. Other photographs document Seth's return from Iraq, graduation, family reunions and birthdays.

Bookshelves ring the room. These shelves hold books that I use on a regular basis to help me minister to those I have been charged to shepherd. I also keep on these shelves mementos of my ministry. I have a jar of sand that I used in a wedding. I keep coffee cups that I have collected around the world from my teaching trips. I have a small plaque that has the cross over the Methodist Flame and the outline of Vietnam.

The walls of my office also reflect my journey through life. One wall is set aside to remind me of my accomplishments. I have a picture of me skydiving, kayaking through ice on Lake Erie, rafting on the New River and one where Home Depot sponsored a kayaking trip across New York State on the Erie Canal.

Behind my desk above the photos are certificates of my spiritual journey. In the middle is my diploma from Houghton College. Next to that is my diploma from United Theological Seminary. Near these are the certificates of my District License from the Wesleyan Church and Commissioning with the United Methodist Church.

My office is similar to many other offices. Our offices help to remind us of where we have been and to help guide us toward a better future. When we have times that we face doubt we need only to look up to see some accomplishments. These offices do help to set the tone that we have worked hard to reach our position or place in business or in ministry.

I believe that Jesus wants us to see the same thing here. Jesus leads us from the throne of God to a room where we are to learn respect. It takes effort on our part to learn how to hallow or respect what God has done for us. Just as you can come into my office to see what I have displayed, we can walk into God's office by merely reading the Bible. These books show God's accomplishments and mementos. All that is recorded is important for us to understand the very nature of God.

We hear God's name around us every day. It has no meaning at all for the world. In fact, it is one of Satan's ploys to devalue God's name. We see it every day, when people get news that is exciting or win a competition; they start to shout, "Oh My God!!"

One show that I have relaxed with on Sunday night is "Home Make Over," a show dedicated to giving families a new start in life with the gift of a new house. I enjoy picking out those who have a personal relationship with Jesus. They are easy to spot when the crowd shouts: "Bus driver, move that bus!" The bus moves aside and for the first time they get to see their new house. In most cases the family runs from room to room shouting "Oh My God!!" Those that have a personal relationship with Jesus have a different attitude. You can see the respect when they say "Oh! My God." You can hear the difference.

Walk down any street or through your workplace and listen. It is used everywhere and with no meaning at all. God has become the familiar. In being familiar we don't think about His awesomeness.

When we begin to read God's message to us we are reminded that it was God that breathed us into existence. It is God that set up the rules of how our Universe spins. Rules like gravity that keeps us grounded.

It is with these rules that someday God will be the Judge. Those that refuse to accept God's love and stay away from God will be judged solely on their actions. Christians, on the other hand, will be judged on how well they followed the commands God gave to us in scripture.

It is God who created the plan for His Son to come to earth to be the ransom for our sins. Even for God this was a great hardship. The Father knew that men would reject Jesus. They would nail him to a tree as a sacrifice. Jesus took all the sin of the world onto his shoulders while nailed to the cross. The sin that he bore was our sin; my sin and yours. It was all the sin that has ever been performed. It was this sin that for a time separated the Son from the Father. This was the true pain for both God and Jesus, the pain of separation. This is why we should put a great importance on God's name and show all the respect that is due.

So how do we Honor His name?

When you have big decisions to make, where do you turn? You seek out those that you trust and have great confidence in. We are to come to the throne of God with boldness and seek his face for help with all of the problems that weigh us down. The ultimate way that we can honor God is through our own lives. We will speak with respect in our homes, our work place, and in all of our relationships with others.

Our world is overwhelming.

Our world is filled with mystery.

Our world causes us to be filled with anxiety. Television shows us the terrors of war, the devastating results of floods, the horrific damage fire creates in families; and television causes our hearts to break when we see the tearstained cheeks of homeless children.

What can we do? Where can we turn?

We can turn to Our Father that is in heaven waiting patiently for us to call upon his Holy Name that we hold in high regard. We can enter with boldness like a son running into his house wanting to tell his dad something exciting or looking to have some hurt healed.

It is by our faith given to us through the Holy Spirit that we can begin to acknowledge our hurts in this world. The Holy Spirit gives to us the comfort and wisdom needed to handle any and all situations.

Father; it is so great to be able to come to you as your child. Remember my brothers and sisters today as we look to you. Let us also remember to keep your name on our lips with respect....Also help us to take the time to search out your word so that we can know more about your character. Help us to desire to learn more about the things you have done for us.

⤙ഐ෬ഐ෬ഐ⤚
SATURDAY
⤙ഐ෬ഐ෬ഐ⤚
(place your reflections on this page)

❧ ✤ ❧ ✤ ❧ ❧ ❧
Sunday
❧ ✤ ❧ ✤ ❧ ❧ ❧
(place your prayer or prayers here)

≪ଈଊଈଊଈଊ୨୬

MONDAY

≪ଈଊଈଊଈଊ୨୬

Stephen shared with us in great detail what his office looks like. If you were to set up an office with unlimited funds what would you place in it?

What inspires you?

Take the time to remember those activities that made you proud of yourself or one of your family members.

List the life events you want to keep some mementos from?

On page 47, Stephen begins to talk about God's office being found in Scripture. List accomplishments in the Bible that God would be directly responsible for.

What pictures would the Triune God hang on the wall? Could you imagine one or more of those frames that allow the pictures to continuously rotate?

Stephen believes that God would have many mementoes collected not only from historical figures in the Bible, but from modern day characters as well.

✦℘ℛ℘ℛ℘ℛ℘℘

TUESDAY

✦℘ℛ℘ℛ℘ℛ℘℘

"We hear God's name around us every day. It has very little or no meaning at all for the world. In fact, it is one of Satan's ploys to devalue God's name." Just as the television show that Stephen mentioned, it is difficult to watch any show without some use of God in a flippant manner.

Okay, so then, it would seem to me, Lee, that we need to find ways to address or combat the implications of Satan's methods. So:

How can we, or what can we, do or say as dedicated Christ followers to show respect for God?

Have we taken the time to examine our lives to see the places where we show disrespect for God?

How do we change, alter, eliminate or modify the bad and limiting actions so that they are altered for the good?

How then do we apply those changes to our daily actions/prayer life as we come to address and relate to God, not with just the *words* "hallowed be thy name," but with a *lifestyle* and *visible actions* that show that we *do* hallow God's name?

55

Stephen again on page 47 wrote that we respect God for what happens in our personal life. Peggy wanted to know if we have the ability to respect God's will regardless of how it affects us. Let us put this in perspective.

How did you feel after the hurricane Katrina blew through the Gulf of Mexico and the numerous towns, villages, and cities? Were you angry, or frustrated, or did you applaud, believing that God was passing judgment?

Does your respect for God depend on your feelings?

I, Stephen, believe that scripture is written in such a way that in our humanness we can understand the spiritual truths found therein. With that disclaimer, God the Father gave his only son to bear our sins on the wooden tree commonly called a cross. Is your respect for God's gift to us diminished in any way by seeing empty crosses everywhere, and things like signs with John 3:16 being hung in stadiums?

Which one of us would ever give up one of their children for someone else's filthy life? I have seven to choose from and I, Stephen, couldn't spare one of them.

Way too often we forget to go to God until we have reached the bottom of the barrel or we are at the end of our rope.

Who have you turned to in times of conflict in your life?

I know that as a pastor I have often said from the pulpit that we are to be the hand and feet of Christ. I have also claimed that we need to be flesh and blood when others need to see Jesus.

When we turn to others, have we first qualified them to be children of God? Have we seen the fruits of the Spirit in their lives?

In this same vane do we look for predetermined answers? Those that we want which fit our plan as we have figured out life to be, or are we willing to allow God to be God and accept the answer that He gives?

How do you wait for the answer? What is your attitude in the waiting?

I, Stephen, have taken it upon myself way too many times to only trust in my own abilities. What about you?

≈ᏍᏳᏣᏍᏳᏣᏍᏳ
FRIDAY
≈ᏍᏳᏣᏍᏳᏣᏍᏳ

Prayer is a conversation with members of the Triune God. How much time are you setting aside each day to have that conversation?

Prayer with God takes time. Have you ever had the goal of getting married? The first thing you do is to look around for someone that interests you, a spark or some chemistry that will draw you together.

Next, once you are past the physical attraction, you will want to spend time getting to know each other. We have the unique gift of speech and hearing. This is the stage where you study each other's movements, likes and dislikes. You want to impress the other person and make very few mistakes. Correct? Of course this is correct.

Something fishy; though, happens at the altar, you have made your catch. Your partner is in the boat, now for some reason you believe the job is done. You can again focus on the things that were once important to you. Sadly, too often our catch gets away. Sadder still, we don't care. We are on to the next thrill of catching another.

Is this a similar story of your love affair with God the Father, Jesus the Son and the Holy Spirit the Sustainer? Get back to work and communicate!!

THE SOLARIUM
GOD'S WINDOW TO THE WORLD

CHAPTER THREE

"Your kingdom come. Your will be done,
on earth as it is in heaven."   Matthew 6:10 NRSV

In a gentler time our grandparents sat out on the front porch to cool off from the day's work and to watch the world go by. Often neighbors would stop to catch up on the news of the family. Times have changed! Now these porches have been removed to the backyard and enclosed to keep the world out. People want to have a view without being too engaged.

God's solarium harkens back to the gentler time. As we move from the Master's Office, we leave with a little more understanding of God's love for humanity. It is with this knowledge that we can truly appreciate moving across the Grand Foyer to the side addition where the solarium rests.

Like most solariums or sunrooms this is a place meant for sitting for a while. The room has a gentle breeze coming in to allow for comfort. Padded seats are placed around for easy conversation. Plants and trees fill in the voids around the room.

The most import aspect to the room; though, is the view out to the world. God the Father, God the Son, and God the Holy Spirit together meet with us to discuss the condition of the world. Also, we find in this room many large windows where God often will bring us over to view his creation of man and earth. It is here in this room that we are invited to hear the plans God has for those in the world. He shows us his innermost desires.

Room with a View
(Thy kingdom come...)

Let's put this first into historical perspective. The Israelites believed that their Messiah or Savior would become an earthly ruler. During the time of Christ the Romans were occupying the land of Israel. Their presence was an insult and oppression. They were feeling a heavy hand on them and were looking for someone that would rise up and release them from bondage. They wanted God's Kingdom on earth in a physical form. That is why it again is a radical departure for Jesus to teach this section of prayer to his disciples.

This tiny phrase sets a new tone of where we fit into God's kingdom. Jesus doesn't suggest that God should enter into our physical world to dance to our agendas or, stated crassly, to be a Santa Claus in our back pocket. This prayer turns us around one hundred and eighty degrees. Jesus leads us to face in a new and different direction that is focused on spiritual matters. We are now expecting to become part of the kingdom of God.

Where is the kingdom of God to be found?

Let us first look at this question like building a home. We need to start with a solid foundation that has strength and can endure the stresses placed upon it.

Our foundation is found within the relations of the Trinity. Jesus laid claim to be the Son of God. Jesus said that he and the Father were one. "If you see me you see the Father." This creates a sense of unity between God, the Father and God the Son. When Jesus was baptized the Spirit of God came upon Jesus. Again scripture says that Jesus was filled with the Spirit after leaving the desert.

This unity found within the Trinity is important to understand because it gives credibility to the very words of Jesus. When Jesus says the "kingdom of God is within you" (Luke 17:20-21) we then can believe that Jesus is speaking for each member of the Trinity.

Jesus came to his own people and claimed to them that the "Kingdom is already among them." How is the kingdom among them? We can further believe that the kingdom of God is within us because in John fifteen Jesus teaches the disciples about God being the vinegrower. Jesus says that if we will abide in him he will abide in us. In other words, Jesus wants to have as close a relationship with us as he has with other members of the Trinity.

Jesus also claims to be the doorway to God, who is in heaven. The first chapter of Acts says that when He left to go back to heaven, Jesus promised that the Holy Spirit would come to dwell in us. It would be an understatement to say the kingdom of God is simply where God presides. Yet, that is the simple truth. The kingdom of God is within us because we accept Christ to be our Savior.

The kingdom of God in this case is not a place or a political regime. This kingdom is a state of being in relationship with the Trinity. Paul, in Romans fourteen: seventeen, puts that the kingdom of God is found in right living, and having peace with joy that comes from the Holy Spirit.

So, how can we tell that the kingdom of God is already here among us? We can tell by the fruit of the Spirit. God the Holy Spirit living in us transforms us so that we begin living a different way. We live for God's will instead of our own.

How does God indwell us? Our lives are transformed on the inside. We begin to see life from a different perspective. We have the power of the Spirit to sustain us. We begin to fall in love with the Triune God more and more.

We also find the kingdom is felt when we meet with other Christians. It can be in our time of corporate worship, or it can be when we are getting together for fun or simply out on the street living life. It is not uncommon to be with someone you just met and know instinctively that they are a sister or brother in Jesus.

How then should we pray?

Let us look out of the window of this room. This is the room where God desires that we agree with Him; that we are looking for his kingdom to be here on earth now.

These words of Jesus; "Your kingdom come, your will be done on earth as it is in heaven" appears to again draw us away from self, but to see God's will for others. I can imagine God calling each one of over to a window and with tears in his eyes asking that we begin to participate with the Trinity in drawing others to the saving knowledge of Jesus so that they too would have the kingdom of God within them.

Together we look out the window and see the world from God's perspective. We now begin to view our friends and families and see their needs from God's perspective. We look out to those that we mix with each day and see what God wants accomplished in their lives.

We look to our town and see it differently. We no longer just drive through seeing trees, houses, and businesses. We now see people that are separated from having an intimate relationship with the Trinity. Together, we now react with sorrow just like God. We also look to our country and our world as a whole. What does God want and how can we be part of it?

After visiting the solarium we are now able to pray for God's kingdom to come to all that we meet. We begin each day with a new perspective. Instead of being focused only on our own issues, we can become excited to see how God can work through us in bringing the kingdom of God to others.

So how do we respond?

Since the kingdom is within us, we need to look inward and honestly examine ourselves. It is time to come before God and ask Him to reveal Himself. We need to allow God to move through our spirit and lay bare any area that we are keeping for ourselves. We need to take off any masks that we are wearing, and open up ourselves to God, so that he can correct our attitudes and our actions. This releases us from our chains and restrictions and allows us to see what God wants to accomplish.

Where do we find God's Will?

We have a personal letter, scripture, written to us from God. In it the Creator explains in great detail how we are to conduct our lives. Scripture is similar to a road map or GPS device that calls out the directions and tells you when you made a wrong turn. It is by learning to lean on each other in small groups that together, we can take on the world and be strong enough to handle it.

We learn about God's "will" by coming together in small groups and taking the time study God's Word. Sometimes that discussion is hard because it begins to illuminate areas of our life that need to be changed. It is during those times that we are uncomfortable that we need to trust in the Holy Spirit to guide us. This is why it is so critical to find a group that you can invest time in so that you become more comfortable sharing your life's journey.

I was part of a small men's group for several years. It was there that I began to sense that God was calling me back into the ministry. My wife, Kristan, had begun to feel that God was calling me back into the ministry. Kristan asked if I would be willing to ask the group if they also felt that this would be God's "will." It took another year of prayer before I was fully committed to the idea. The Lord opened doors for our family as soon as I opened myself up to God's calling.

Several years later my friend Craig, who was part of this small group, also felt the call on his life to enter full time service. I asked if he would be willing to walk with me in ministry. So, today we serve several churches together.

Remember that heaven is inside of us. Once we have ourselves in balance, and are looking for God's will, we can then reach out to those we see out of God's window.

God wants us to bring His heavenly will to those that are around us here on earth. We are again being asked to touch other lives for the furtherance of the kingdom of God. He wants us to infect everything that is around us. I now have the opportunity to become the hands and feet of God in Vietnam. The United Methodist Church there is beginning to answer the call. House churches are popping up everywhere. People's lives are being transformed. I have been able to work with a team from United Theological Seminary that is teaching local pastor's how to share the Good News. The church has been growing through the working of the Holy Spirit.

Through God working in us we then can reach out to the hurting world around us. It is then that His kingdom comes. His will be done, on earth, as in heaven. Today let us make a commitment to pray as God would have us to pray, and to look out the window into his hurting world. Let us make the difference in someone else's life.

Father; it is so great to be able to come to you as your child. Remember my brothers and sisters today as we look to you. Let us also remember to keep your name on our lips with respect....

Let us become a partner with you in reaching those that are lost and hurting. Help us bring your kingdom to them so that they too can become your children...

≼ଈଔଈଔଈଔ୬

SATURDAY

≼ଈଔଈଔଈଔ୬

(place your reflections on this page)

❦❧❦❧❦❧❦

Sunday

❦❧❦❧❦❧❦

(place your prayer or prayers here)

This prayer is so radical because its fulfillment of the kingdom is the direct opposite of what the Israelite nation was looking for. We have read that the Jewish people were being taken over by other nations because of their disobedience to their God, Yahweh.

Can you make a list of the different rulers that invaded the nation of Israel?

With each of these different rulers taking over the land and taking the people into captivity, can you recall any of the specific circumstances that caused their downfall? This is a good place to search the internet for the answer.

When you complete this list you will have a greater understanding that when the Israelites were looking for the kingdom of God, they were looking for political revenge.

※℘ℭℜ℘ℭℜ℘ℊ
TUESDAY
※℘ℭℜ℘ℭℜ℘ℊ

Jesus does allow for the physical kingdom of Heaven where God does sit on a throne. This is a final destination for those who have accepted Jesus as their Lord and Savior. Luke chapter twelve is where Jesus gives us great insight into this future kingdom.

Read verses 13-34 to see that is better to work toward a future in heaven where thieves cannot steal your treasure. What treasure can we store in Heaven?

What do you make of verse 40?

You can compare this with the ten bridesmaids in Matthew 25:1-13. What is this story about?

Do you believe that some people will not make it into heaven? It would seem so.

So then, what must we be doing each day to have our lamps lit?

Now that we understand that there is a heaven to come, what does it mean then that the Kingdom of God is at hand or within? Read these three passages to find a fuller understanding.

Matthew 12:23-28, Mark 1:14-15, Mark 12:28-34

Mathew 12 – In this passage Jesus was talking about how a kingdom divided wouldn't stand or last. What do you think Jesus meant when he said if he were to cast out the demon the kingdom has come?

Is this a future event or a current event? Who or what fills the void of the demon?

Mark 1 – What had been fulfilled?

Is the kingdom related to the presence of Jesus?

Mark 12 – What did Jesus mean that the man was not far from the kingdom?

Was this person about to believe in Jesus as the Savior?

eocreocreo

THURSDAY

eocreocreo

How do I "hear the plans God has for those in the world?"

How do I "infect" someone?

How do I set up a plan to do these things today?

Here I, Lee, have the age-old lament: "But tell me what to *do*."

Are we talking about a more direct action to mention Christ outright, or direct someone in a more Christ-oriented direction? Am I talking here about overt evangelism as opposed to "making a difference in someone else's life", which may be in a less direct approach to someone's salvation—I think.

Return to Mark 12:30-31 to see that to find God's will first start with loving God with all that you have. Next is to love others in the same way. When these are at the bottom of all of our actions wouldn't we be seeking the best for others?

≪৩৩০৫৩০৫৩০৬
Friday
≪৩৩০৫৩০৫৩০৬

So how can we tell when the kingdom is within us? It would seem that if we had the kingdom within us something would be different? If the Spirit of the Living God lived in us we ought to be different? If the same Spirit who was in Jesus during his ministry on earth is in us we ought to have some of the same results? Right? Of course, right.

Galatians 5:22-26 is a great place to start.

Love, joy, peace, patience, kindness, generosity, faithfulness, gentleness, and self-control are all fruits of the Spirit. Can you imagine finding these qualities in those not controlled by the Spirit? Sure, for a period of time. It is also noteworthy to say that if one is filled with the Spirit it may take a lifetime to master each of these fruits.

Describe what the world is normally like and do these fruits fit the picture?

THE KITCHENS

&

STORE ROOMS

CHAPTER FOUR

Give us each day our daily bread.
Luke 11:3 NRSV

In this chapter we are leaving the elegant rooms that Jesus first led us too. We leave behind the Grand Foyer where God, the Creator, sits upon the Throne of Glory. It is in that awe inspiring room that God expects to meet with us regularly on a daily basis. We also leave behind the Master's Office where we were allowed to witness glorious achievements, special mementos, and framed photos of all God's Children. We truly saw that Jehovah is to be held in high esteem. We leave the Solarium where together, God the Father and his children look out over the Kingdom. It is here that God shares with us the dreams and desires the Trinity has for those they love and care for.

These three great rooms helped us to focus our attention on the spiritual side of our relationship with the Triune God. Jesus, in this prayer, also recognizes our physical needs as well. It is only after we have met with the Triune God and have taken the time to care for the needs of others around us that we can begin to think of our needs.

Kitchens, Storerooms and also a meditation room

Jesus, in this prayer that is becoming our pattern, stays consistent with giving the disciples a message with multiple implications. When we take time to break down Luke 11:3 we can see that Jesus is meaning more than what meets the eye at first glance. We leave behind the great rooms that have tremendous beauty. We now go down to the bottom floors where the kitchen and storerooms are found. Behind all of the glitz and glamour of every mansion, we know that somewhere out of sight there are common rooms that supply the household needs.

Imagine with me how many guests of Oprah Winfrey, Tom Hanks, Jack Nicholas, or any other famous celebrities have been allowed to descend below the public areas to see where all of the cleaning supplies are kept, the food is kept, or where the meals are made. Guests see only what is grand and beautiful.

Now that we are children of God we are no longer considered guests of our heavenly father. We are instead his beloved children that have the entire run of the home that Jesus had prepared especially for each one of us. We not only to go places that are set aside for guests in the beautiful ornate areas, but now we frequent those areas that are common and ordinary. In fact, we chose to hang out there. Isn't true today the most common place in our homes is the kitchen table to hang out with friends and family.

Each item of food, clothing or supply that is hidden down in these rooms has truly become important or essential to our daily existence. One place at my home that I am always sneaking into is the pantry, especially, when I am craving something salty or sugary to eat. In this small room one can find all of the basic cooking ingredients for delicious dishes. Shelves line the walls with many of our favorite items set up in neat little rows. In a palace or a mansion, the chef is always on call to meet the master's culinary desire. Due to the need to always be at the ready, the shelves have to be fully stocked at all times with the master's favorite ingredients.

Next to the pantry would be the walk-in cooler and the freezers to supply all of the other necessary ingredients. In fact, taking care of the master's needs is only part of the equation. The master regularly holds parties and expects that the guests are well taken care of additionally. The storerooms must also be on the ready to take care of those in need from disasters or for those being oppressed.

The kitchen continuously draws us in because of the delicious smells coming from the various dishes; such as bread and chocolate cookies. This room always provides comfort to the soul with the warmth coming off the ovens. As we enter, the cook always has a place for us to sit where we can talk about our daily activities and those areas of life that concern us. We can keep our hands busy with little tasks, such as peeling the carrots or slicing the potatoes.

The storerooms and the kitchen are meant to supply our physical needs. Jesus in this prayer also is concerned for our daily spiritual needs. So, in an out of the way place, behind the storerooms, is a small room with a heavy door. Behind this door is special place that has enough room for one. At the end of this room is an altar with candles and incense burning.

Look around and you will notice there are no chairs or benches. Only at the altar is a place to kneel. This room was designed to be a quiet place where the world is kept out. On the walls of this room are shelves filled with books, designed to give encouragement and enlightenment.

The first book that is always open to us is the Word of God, the Bible. God has inspired many different authors to write on the things of God and how to live in this world. God provides these scriptures to fill our mind with wisdom that will help to guide our thoughts, and to lead us into a deeper relationship with Him.

The God of the Universe cares about our daily existence. He cares that we have enough to eat, clothes to wear, and that our spiritual life is kept up. These rooms that Jesus has prepared for us are necessary and they are always open to us.

Be it either spiritual or physical help we need from God, it is our responsibility to seek and to ask for help. Too often the expectation is that these items should just be given to us. In Luke, after Jesus taught this prayer to the disciples, he began to speak about how a person who had gone to bed had a surprise visitor. It was common for the host to offer food to a guest. Unfortunately, this host had none available. So he ran next door to get some food from his neighbor. As you can expect the neighbor was none too happy to be awakened at night. It wasn't his friend that had come. He was well tucked in for the night and he wasn't afraid to express it. Yet, the man with the guest would not stop asking for a hand out of food.

Jesus is quoted as saying; "Ask and it will be given to you, if you search you will be rewarded with finding it, and if you knock long enough the door will be opened to you." In the twelfth chapter of Luke, Jesus also gives this advice, "you must first seek the kingdom" or, in other words, seek God's will for the situation. If your request is then in the will of God what you ask for will be given to you.

We are to be seeking what God wants. Yes, we have the kingdom within us. Yet, we are to continually seek a deeper relationship with our Father. We start with the spiritual before we can begin to think about the physical. We need to have daily nourishment of the spiritual food as well as the physical food.

Our Physical Needs

Jesus in this practical prayer is teaching the disciples that it is only through the Father that we receive our physical and spiritual nourishment. When we were following the world's wisdom, before we heard the Holy Spirit calling to us, we relied on our own abilities to provide for all of our needs. The truth becomes revealed to us that our life, our skills and abilities, and our daily substance come only from God who created us.

Several years back I was speaking in New Mexico at a conference for camp directors. I had arrived a couple of days early and had time to explore Santa Fe. In the museum district there was a mall where the local artisans displayed their works. Paintings hung from the walls. Sculptures were scattered around on pedestals and some were on the floor.

One sculpture grabbed my attention. It illustrated a man breaking free from a block of marble. In one hand the man had a hammer and in the other hand a chisel. He was working hard to break himself free from the stone that held him captive. I stood there for a long time working out how this could even be possible. The look of satisfaction on his face gave me the impression that it was out of his own determination and his own ability that he was able to set himself free.

However, when I looked beyond what was shown it was evident that someone else was required to give this man a start. He did not, out of his own free will, begin. The artisan had to start the process. In all reality, no matter what the artisan showed to us, it was entirely the artist's doing.

Like this stone man breaking loose, we have to be reminded where our abilities come from. It is then and only then that we can thank God for all that we have.

Jesus didn't give this prayer so that the disciples would sit back and wait for God to give them their daily rations of food, housing and life sustaining items. Each day Jesus modeled that we must also perform our part of the spiritual bargain. God has given us a great gift to come along side Him to help create with our God given talents, abilities, and a mind with which to create. We get to participate in the world that He gave to us to manage. We are free to be all that God has created within us and to explore our limits. It is a gift not to be enclosed in stone, but free to express ourselves.

God works in conjunction with the real world to provide for real needs.

Jesus began his ministry in his home town of Nazareth. It was there in the synagogue on the Sabbath, as was his tradition that he was asked to read from the scroll of Isaiah. The reading that day set out a clear agenda for his mission to reach out to those around him. It was that mission that Jesus modeled for us. This is found in Luke chapter four.

It is in this model that we need to look further at our responsibility to this world. We have established that we are the children of God that have been invited to come into the Solarium to view God's will for this world. Jesus opens up to us in this mission of God's will for him as well as for us in this statement. We are to become the champion to those who are oppressed. We have the ability with our talents and gifts to give aid to the poor (and those poor in spirit.) Jesus sends us into horrible and even dangerous places to give hope to those who have none.

People are held captive to life with its snares. We are also called to aid those who are blind to the true conditions that they are in. Jesus calls us to give physical aid to those who need first before they are open to their spiritual needs.

We are not isolated islands that are only responsible for ourselves and those close to us. We have grown accustomed to letting the world take care of others and their needs. In America we have allowed the government programs to take care of those that we have been charged to assist.

God also calls for social justice. Why do we have a welfare program and a Medicaid program or any program that the government wants to put a name to? We have it because the 'Church' has run from its responsibilities. God calls for us to take care of the widows, the orphans, and those that are unable to fend for themselves.

Let us take this mantle back on ourselves. Let us begin to seek out those that are less fortunate than we are. If we are to receive the gifts from God that we feel are due to us, we need to first seek God's Kingdom and see what God's Will is. We have been given much and it is good stewardship to return a portion back to God's work. Trust me in this, you will have more joy than you can imagine, especially if the gift is directed with a specific purpose. It is easy to drop money into the offering plate or into a red kettle. It takes time and energy to take food to a neighbor, or to seek out the hurting, or to pay for a heating bill.

Father; it is so great to be able to come to you as your child. Remember my brothers and sisters today as we look to you. Let us also remember to keep your name on our lips with respect....

Let us become a partner with you in reaching those that are lost and hurting. Help us bring your kingdom to them so that they too can become your children...

Help us to recognize that we are not an island. We need the help of others to provide for our daily provisions. Thank you for allowing us to be part of your creative world. You alone give us the talents and the abilities so that we can provide for our families. In turn, Father, help us to be aware of those around us that are less fortunate than we are. Help us to take time to provide for others....

⊰ℬ⟩ℛℬ⟩ℛℬ⟩ℬ⊱
SATURDAY
⊰ℬ⟩ℛℬ⟩ℛℬ⟩ℬ⊱
(place your reflections on this page)

&ଔଔଔ୬

Sunday

&ଔଔଔ୬

(place your prayer or prayers here)

MONDAY

We have governments that create laws that govern our world. It is from these laws that some have freedom to expand, while others are destined to poverty. Take time to pray for our government officials that God's will would be done.

People have been empowered to enforce these laws. Police and Judges need our prayers so that they will not become biased or corrupted so that God's will can be accomplished.

Pray for the soldiers in the Armed Services that they will serve to protect those that cannot protect themselves. It is then that God can move in a mighty way.

Pray for those that raise our food. Pray for those that make our clothes. Pray for those that provide our utilities so that we have heat and power to run our many electronic devices. We do not live on an island. God works through so many to provide our 'Daily Bread'. This list could go on and on.

How far beyond the daily allotment of nourishment does this request extend?

Can it extend?

Does it extend?
How do you feel about having God seen as a Santa Claus?

I, Stephen, was trapped for many years in the idea that God was to give us great riches. I read the Prayer of Jabez and claimed it all the way to a credit card debt of several years' income.

The chapter seems to hint at much more: We get to participate in the world that He gave us. We get to explore our limits. We are free to be all that God has created within us. It is a gift to not be enclosed in stone, but to be free to express ourselves. What do we do with our own hammer and chisel to break free and "Be all that we can be?"

91

≪⁂⁂⁂⁂≫
WEDNESDAY
≪⁂⁂⁂⁂≫

Stephen in yesterday's lesson mentioned the prayer of Jabez, this would be a good place to start today. Please read I Chronicles 4:9-10. These two verses seem to be out of place with the surround text, wouldn't you agree?

How would you like the name Jabez. It would seem that it would be a terrible reminder of the day that he was born. We can only imagine what caused his mother to have so much pain, but she wanted to be reminded of it all day long every day. Can you hear her calling out to him, she would say, "'Because I had so much pain' get your butt in here!"

During his life; though, Jabez became honored above his brothers. At some point in his life he called out to God and dared to ask some of the same things that concern us today. He wanted his life to be easier. He wanted to increase his earning potential when he wanted more land. These things in themselves are not evil. God would agree, because He honored Jabez's prayer.

So, where have we twisted this world to only look to God for personal riches? Is this where we find our fulfillment?

THURSDAY

What are you asking God for Today? Have you come with the attitude of "our" or "my"?

This not to say that we are not to come to God with personal desires, needs, and even wants. It is; though, a reminder of the need to find the focus of what to pray for. So often we desire a life free from pain and misery. It has become a calling card of some evangelists to present this kind of lifestyle, but what does God say?

This is a place for you to truly take the time to search scripture. I also encourage you to find books on the proper use of money and stewardship of God's world.

The danger for me and the team here is to provide some verses that would only present a narrow picture of the true blessing of living under God's desire for us to live well. I would like to lift up that it is more important to live a life full of spiritual and relational treasure rather than chasing after things that will only temporarily make us happy.

&⁊⊃⊂⊗⊃⊂⊗⊃&
FRIDAY
&⁊⊃⊂⊗⊃⊂⊗⊃&

After reading so far, Stephen wants to know how you are going to seek God's kingdom first.

Make a commitment to take time for God. Find that small room and go there regularly to receive your daily spiritual nourishment.

Be thankful for the gift of your ability to earn your living so that your family is provided for.

Be aware of those in need around you so that you can be part of God's work in providing for their daily needs.

In all things, do them with great joy of heart.

THE MUDROOM & WASHROOM

CHAPTER FIVE

And forgive us our sins, for we ourselves forgive everyone indebted to us.

Luke 11:4a (NRSV)

The Family Entrance is not the one found out front. It is not the one with the golden doors that lead directly into the Grand Foyer. These doors are not the doors for our entrance. Those doors are reserved for bringing our guests just as Jesus brought us. Those doors are also for those special occasions where we need to have quick access to the Father because we are in great distress.

Remember now that we are family. We have become heirs to this kingdom, due to the fact that we are the children of God. Our family entrance is around to the side near the stables.

Rooms for Cleanliness

As we enter through this side door, we come into a common or humble room with many hooks and pegs. With a family so large it is necessary for all of these hooks so that all of the family can hang up their work coats and hats. There are comfortable chairs about where we can relax as we take off our muddy boots and dirty clothes. Near the mudroom you'll find the washroom. These two rooms allow the family members to become presentable as they enter the rest of the house. The names on the outside of these two rooms are forgiveness, mercy and grace. Family members must pass this way and do so often.

It wouldn't be acceptable to sit at the dinner table with muddy boots, dirty clothes and unwashed hands. God provided these rooms so that when we enter we are renewed, refreshed and cleansed. We become soiled daily by the real world that we live in.

Jesus, in his model prayer, gives each one of us the chance to come to God to face our sins or shortcomings with an open and honest heart. We do not have to be like Adam and Eve and hide from God. He loves us so much that he prepared a room so that we could become clean and presentable. Look with me again to Luke eleven.

"And forgive us our sins for we ourselves forgive everyone indebted to us."
Luke 11:4 (NRSV)

Our Father knows the world that we live in. He knows that our flesh is not capable of resisting all temptations. Our Creator has prepared a way for us that we can daily find his mercy and forgiveness. Our part is to come to Him with an honest heart, open to his correcting.

The Parable of the Two Servants

It is critical for our understanding of this passage to see that the first part of the verse is dependent on the second half. Our forgiveness is based on our ability to forgive those who have sinned against us. This has caused me to wrestle with God many times. I want to raise my fist in anger and ask God how I can forgive "that" sin. It cut me so badly that I am not sure if I can recover. This is truly where the rubber meets the road.

"for we ourselves forgive everyone indebted to us."
Luke 11:4 (NRSV)

Do you recall the story Jesus told of the two servants? Each of these servants owed a debt. The first servant owed a huge amount to his king. Yet, the king looked down with kindness and with compassion. He said to his servant that his entire bill was paid off.

Has anyone treated you this way? Think back to that time. How did it feel? In truth, if you accepted Christ into your life, you have the largest debt ever paid off.

Now this freed man went out into the street and saw a man that owed him about a week's worth of wages. He refused to learn the lesson given to him just a few moments before. He turned on this man with his full vengeance and demanded his money. You know the rest of the story. The king heard the story and brought him back for an explanation. In the end, he put this forgiven man into jail until he could pay off his debt.

Let's go back to the mudroom where we can watch the rest of our family coming and going. Look as they come in. They are taking off their outer coats. These coats are heavy and soiled with the sins that have been committed against our brothers and sisters. As we watch we can see that sometimes they are struggling with the weight of these coats. Look at their faces, though. When they finally get these coats off they feel that a great burden has been lifted off. What is happening is that they are taking the time to forgive others for what has been done to them. It takes time to intentionally forgive. This is a deliberate act that they perform every time they come into the room. They need to get rid of this cloak before they can begin to receive the cleansing given to them by the blood of Jesus. Matthew 6:14 &15 confirm to us that we need to first forgive others before God can forgive us of our sins.

It is only after we have humbled ourselves that we can face Jesus to receive our cleansing. The mudroom was the place set aside for us to take care of the business of forgiving others. It is only through the work of the Holy Spirit in us that we have the power to offer this forgiveness.

King David becomes a living example

King David led a life that caused him to come continually before God for forgiveness. Read David's prayer as he sought God in Psalm 32:1-11. David goes directly to his Creator giving praise because his Lord God had coved his sins and no longer counted them against him. This prayer foreshadows the grace given to us by Christ's death on the cross where our sins are washed clean to the point we are as pure as snow.

David came to the washroom only after having come through the mudroom. After he took off his muddy boots, and soiled clothes, he gave these over to God as confessions.

Jesus, in his mercy washes each one of us clean as we come seeking forgiveness of our sins. David sets the example for us to come to Jesus asking for forgiveness of our sins Then Jesus is faithful in the action of cleansing us. God the Father only sees our humanity through the lens of Jesus and the action on the cross. We are pure, clean, spotless, and sin free. Jesus took upon himself our sins at the cross. Not just sin in general, but each sin that has ever been committed by everyone. Our part is to be thankful and humbled by this action for us. We need to have a heart that breaks because of our action.

After having been cleaned thoroughly we will run through the house singing with joy that we have been washed clean like David.

Father; it is so great to be able to come to you as your child. Remember my brothers and sisters today as we look to you. Let us also remember to keep your name on our lips with respect....

Let us become a partner with you in reaching those that are lost and hurting. Help us bring your kingdom to them so that they too can become your children...

Help us to recognize that we are not an island. We need the help of others to provide for our daily provisions. Thank you for allowing us to be part of your creative world. You alone give us the talents and the abilities so that we can provide for our families. In turn Father help us to be aware of those around us that are less fortunate than we are. Help us to take time to provide for others....

Keep us forever mindful that we first must take the time to take off the coat of unforgiveness and place it on a hook for Christ to deal with. Let us enter often the rooms provided for us to become clean from the sins of the world....

SATURDAY

(place your reflections on this page)

◈ℰℭℛℰℭℛℰℭℛℰℭℛ◈

Sᴜɴᴅᴀʏ

◈ℰℭℛℰℭℛℰℭℛℰℭℛ◈

(place your prayer or prayers here)

Monday

King David's life story has inspired people down through the ages. It is surprising that Hollywood hasn't adopted him as an official mascot for their action-packed thrillers. He did it all from his early childhood. He received the king's daughter by killing a giant. Enemy soldiers went to bed each night ready to face the nightmares in their dreams because of the terror David caused on the battle field. King Saul had his thousands that he killed, while David had his tens of thousands. David lost his battle with temptation when he saw a beautiful woman taking a bath. She lost her husband on the front lines because King David wanted him out of the way.

Even with all that David did against the will of God, he continuously fell on his face to seek God's forgiveness.

Now it's your turn **to daily** take off your outer cloak let it remind you that once you were held down with a heavy burden of sin. It is time to place that sin or cloak up on the hook and begin the process of giving forgiveness to those who have sinned against you. Enjoy that feeling in your shoulder as the weights are being lifted off. Enter into the washroom where you meet with Christ to ask for your forgiveness of your sin so that he can cleanse you. It is nothing that you can do on your own. It is only through the grace of the Holy Spirit working in you that you can be forgiven.

As we move into today's lesson let us go back to yesterday and revisit King David. King David didn't have the consequences of this sin removed. One of his sons wanted his kingdom and found a way to have him discredited. King David had to run for his life.

What King David did have was an inner peace that comes from God's forgiveness. We saw also the consequences of sin in the story of the two servants. The servant with the most to lose couldn't transfer the same forgiveness to the one who owed so little.

What do you think caused this hard heart?

Where are you in this story?

How was it when God forgave you?
Did you feel the world come off your shoulders?

Are you giving others the same grace that Jesus gave you?
How little is their debt in comparison?

WEDNESDAY

What is forgiveness and why must we have it?

In many ways this question is too broad and the answer begins and ends with how God is present in our lives. Our relationship first begins with God's desire to be in a personal relationship with not just humanity, but with each and every one individually. See Ephesians 1:2-6 and also Genesis 1:26.

We were created with a spirit nature to be in this relationship with God who is spirit. With an all knowing God, the Creator knew that we would become sinful in our nature and turn our backs on God. Therefore in God's wisdom a plan was made for us to be literally saved from ourselves. Within that plan God provided "Grace" for us.

What is Grace? Before the explanation look at Ephesians 2:4-9, Grace can be best defined as: "the loving actions of the Triune God that are undeserved and unmerited." In verse 8, Paul says that it is not by our doing, but by God's. Verse 9 further clarifies that it is not by works

God's Plan – Jesus, the son of God, was sent to earth to become our sacrifice for our sins. John 3: 16-21

≪⁓ᔄᗧᔄᗧᔄ⁓≫
THURSDAY
≪⁓ᔄᗧᔄᗧᔄ⁓≫

Yesterday's lesson gave insight into God's love for us and the gift of "Grace." In the scripture lesson of John, we see that Jesus had to sacrifice his life for ours. In this lesson we will unpack this gift from Romans 6:1-18.

For me, Stephen, I love the entire concept of baptism. This is one area of our faith where we can put a tactile experience with a spiritual event. When we come to Christ to receive him as Lord of our life, it is done within one's heart (and mind.) Yet, this action is done with water and with people around fully participating either by accepting responsibility or joining in the celebration. Let me point out one danger, many individuals feel that it had been their decision to become baptized. This flies in the face of "Grace." The Holy Spirit calls to us and leads to this point allowing oneself to be baptized.

What denomination (if any) you are part of will influence the method of baptism. Some merely sprinkle, which I do most, or some fully immerse the person under the water. Either way the same action is being taken by the Spirit of God. This is simply an outward sign of an inward activity.

The symbolism is awesome; we die with Christ as we are being lowered into the water (or being sprinkled). It is here that are sins are being washed away. We come up with a new life in Christ. We are new creatures, not just remade and shifting things around. We have been transformed into the image of Christ.

Look at verse 5; what do you believe this to mean?

Is this current?
Does this go back in time to his resurrection?
This is a verse that should be read in many different translations. Some would also point to a future time.
How does this affect you?

Look at verse 6; this is the verse that you can count on knowing that you are forgiven.

What does it mean to be no longer a slave to sin?

Does that mean that you will sin no more?
If that were true, it would make life easier.

What does it mean then?

This is all about one's focus. We now accept the forgiveness of Jesus and begin to focus our love and attention on learn more about the Triune God. It is about courtship and falling in love.

~&€)(8€)(8€)~
FRIDAY
~&€)(8€)(8€)~

You thought you had turned your pain over to God. You thought your emotional wounds were behind you. Suddenly though with a word, a smell, a sound, or some trigger it all came rushing back to you. You had placed this hurt deep down inside of you and now its back. You again have to deal with the act of forgiving someone. Maybe, just maybe, you are in the middle of going through a fresh incident.

We all have been wounded in some way. How have your wounds shaped your life?

I am sure that some may question God where he was during this time. Read Psalms 33:18-22, Proverbs 15:3
What do you think now about God?
Is this tough to deal with – the read Romans 12:19-21
Is this as easy as it sounds?

We want more than justice. We want revenge for what has happened to us. Question – if God is all knowing and desires to have the very best for us – How then can we question God? Have you ever known revenge to work?

How is it that our forgiveness is so critical? Have you led a perfect life that you have caused no harm?
For more in-depth studies on this go to www.nooma.com
Look up lesson 007 Luggage

109

Replenishing the Storeroom at the Store

Chapter Six

Candy Bar, Bags of Chips, and Ho Ho's!
Temptation just a reach away!

"And lead us not into temptation, but deliver us from the evil one." Matthew 6:13. (NIV)

Like any normal day I wander into the kitchen for breakfast. It doesn't take long to notice that we are a tad bit low on supplies; especially milk. I can't live without cold milk: the colder the better. So, with cash in hand, I head off to the store. Forgetting an age old saying, "never go shopping on an empty stomach."

Even before I get to the grocery store I can feel my stomach gnawing and turning. Pulling into the parking lot begins the gauntlet of temptations. I swear that these stores have learned selling techniques from Disney. Wafting through the air is an inviting smell of fresh donuts and other fattening creations. When I was a contractor years ago I put an addition on a grocery store. During the course of that year I gained twenty pounds.

I learned to skip breakfast at home so I could eat a couple of donuts upon my arrival. It wasn't long before the ten o'clock break, and I needed to fill up on more donuts and fresh black coffee. Half way through the construction of this addition I was finding my way back to the deli for lunch as well. So, with that being said, the parking lot is always my first fight against temptation. Oh, I wish I was an Amish horse on an old country road. Those Amish farmers know that they need to put blinders over their horse's eyes to keep them on the road.

Who needs a shopping list? I do, I normally keep the list in my hand so that I can keep on task. It seems that at the end of each isle is a rack of chips. Small bags, medium sized bags, large bags, variety pack bags, and family sized bags. Most of the time I do well passing these by, but sometimes if the hunger monster strikes, those bags of kettle cooked salt and vinegar chips just fall into my cart. If I am really bad this bag may not make it home. It wouldn't break my heart if some cheesy puffs fell in too.

With check marks on all the items on my list I make a mad dash for the registers only to be confronted with the store's last stand. I take it that some individuals must be tempted with knowing the latest gossip on who is dating who and who is pregnant and by whom. So, there sits the glossy magazines like moths many are drawn into their next purchase. I, on the other hand, nearly have to put my hands in my pockets not to pick up a candy bar, a sucker or one of those lip smacking sour powder dispensers.

Temptation, it is everywhere. It is how we come to handle temptation that is critical. Years later I am still paying for those intoxicating donuts. Talk about consequences to our sinful actions. I am learning to love the weight machines. In fact, Kristan put one on our porch so I have to look at it every day.

Let's look back to our model prayer in Matthew.

"And lead us not into temptation, but deliver us from the evil one." Matthew 6:13. (NIV)

To some the phase "lead us not into temptation" is in direct opposition to the rest of scripture. Scripture tells us that God does not and cannot tempt us (James 1:13.) The next verse says that it is our own desires at work.

So, then, what do we do with this model of prayer that Jesus has given to us? Was Jesus wrong or misleading the disciples?

Can Jesus have made a mistake?

Or is it that the Bible has mismatched sayings and not to be considered true and perfect?

No, the problem is with our American view of the world around us. We look at scripture from our experiences, and from our setting. Rarely do we slow down to look at events from other people's perspective. Kristan and I both went to Houghton Academy where the student body was made up with Americans but also a large percentage of students who came from various countries around the world. Kristan's parents hosted a girl from China one year. After one dinner while the girl's father was visiting, the family was sitting around the table and the man from China let out a huge burp. This took Kristan's family by surprise. Apparently they didn't hide it well since the girl ended up explaining in China it is a sign of respect for the cook. Our ways are not always the right way, and it doesn't make it wrong for others to act in a different way.

So, how do we take this phrase? First, understand that the Bible was not written in English. Jesus did not speak in King James or in any other translation. The Bible was written in some places in Hebrew and in other places in Greek. These words, then, have to be translated through time and through history. Sometimes the translation can only come close to the original meaning.

The Hebrew word for temptation used here is **massâh** (*mas-saw'*): a *testing* of men similar to a judicial trial.

The Greeks have used two different words in their translation.

The first being; **pagis** (*pag-ece'*)a *trap;* figuratively a *trick* or *stratagem* or a snare.

The second application is **peirasmos** (*pi-ras-mos'*) a putting to *proof* by experiment, *experience*, solicitation, discipline or provocation.

The English word temptation is from the Latin and originally meant trials whether good or bad, but the evil sense has monopolized the word in our modern English.

Don't zone out on me here. It is important to understand what the original words of Jesus were and how they fit into this prayer. Jesus is talking about going through a trial or a test. The Book of James, found in the

115

New Testament, explains why it is important for us to go through trials and tests. James was writing to his friends and wanted to let them know that, even though they felt they were having it rough with temptations or trials, they were fortunate. It is through the trials and testing with faith and endurance that one is made perfect, complete, and will lack nothing in the end. James 1:2-4)

Coaches are notorious for putting their players through trial after relentless trial. When I played soccer the coach had us each day do the same drills over and over again. One reason is that we were never perfect. The coach could see our mistakes. He would then point them out to us, show us how to do it better and then have us practice the drill again. Why all this effort? So that, when it came to game day and it mattered, we were prepared and ready for whatever the opposition sent our way.

God does the same thing for us. He will send tests our way to so that we can practice our skills. In Matthew Jesus shows us the actual competition between himself and Satan. Jesus went to the desert to pray and fast after he was baptized by John in the Jordon River. After forty days, Satan came to test him. With each attack Jesus used scripture to press Satan back. He knew that the scripture that Satan used was being taken out of context and manipulated to make his point. Jesus was able to counter each attack with God's words found in scripture that were true and accurate.

Look at the phrase again - "And lead us not into temptation." What does this mean then? It means, "Father do not put us to trial before we are ready." So, many Christians fail their tests. Why? Because they fail to prepare themselves for action. We expect that God should do everything for us. Look back to the perfect example provided for us in scripture. When Jesus was being tempted he had the answers. Why, because he was practiced up. We can see Jesus as he was growing up, that he took the time to learn about scripture, and actively put it to the test.

When he was twelve Joseph and Mary took him to Jerusalem to celebrate the Passover. On the way home, Mary noticed that Jesus was not with them. When they returned to the city they looked everywhere and finally found Jesus in the Temple talking with the priests. They were amazed at his knowledge of scripture, and the questions that he asked. Jesus made it a point to study scripture, and then put it into practice by talking about it.

Today, we need to follow the example that Jesus gave us. We need to daily get into his word, so that, when the time comes we have learned scripture to defend ourselves. I find it extremely encouraging that this is a team sport. Jesus again puts into the phrase the one small word "us." And lead **"us"** not into temptation. We are to practice together. It is important that like the soccer team, we get together on a regular basis and practice our skills. So, when it comes time for the big test, we will be prepared.

The second part explains who does the tempting. Again, look back to Matthew 6:13 (NIV).

"but deliver us from the evil one."

Satan is out to destroy you any way that he can. He knows you better than you know yourselves. He and his legions study your weaknesses so that they can attack you. This is where the Greek translation fits best. Satan and his team are actively trying to trap or snare you. We are good most of the time recognizing the big temptations, but he is great at sneaking us those little temptations.

"It is just one donut, what can it hurt." For me one just wasn't enough. If you ever drive through South Dayton, New York, don't stop at the bakery. Satan lives there. They make the best donuts that I have ever had. First, they are huge and filled with jars full of filling. Often, when you buy a jelly donut at one of the drive through donut shops you wonder where the filling is. Not in South Dayton, the filling spills out onto your fingers and falls all over yourself. If you stop make sure you have plenty of napkins and water to clean up with.

Scripture describes Satan like a thief that will come in the night or like a roaring lion in 1Peter 5:8 you are warned to be on you guard, because the Devil is roaming around like an angry lion looking for its next meal.

In bringing this all together, we need to pray that God will not allow Satan to attack us before we are ready to defeat him. We need to become so involved with each other in our practice that when the tests come from our enemy we are prepared.

Father; it is so great to be able to come to you as your child. Remember my brothers and sisters today as we look to you. Let us also remember to keep your name on our lips with respect....

Let us become a partner with you in reaching those that are lost and hurting. Help us bring your kingdom to them so that they too can become your children...

Help us to recognize that we are not an island. We need the help of others to provide for our daily provisions. Thank you for allowing us to be part of your creative world. You alone give us the talents and the abilities so that we can provide for our families. In turn Father help us to be aware of those around us that are less fortunate than we are. Help us to take time to provide for others....

Keep us forever mindful that we first must take the time to take the coat of unforgivingness off and place it on a hook for Christ to deal with. Let us enter often the rooms provided for us to become clean from the sins of the world....

Father I know that a time for the big test is coming. Help me to prepare for this battle with my fellow travelers. Keep the evil one at bay until we are prepared. Thank you for your guidance and wisdom as we learn more about your ways...

❦❧❦❧❦❧❦❧

SATURDAY

❦❧❦❧❦❧❦❧

(place your reflections on this page)

≼ॐ৳ॐ৳ॐ৸

Sunday

≼ॐ৳ॐ৳ॐ৸

(place your prayer or prayers here)

Stephen was pretty open about some of his temptations. The truth is these were just the short list. If we become honest with ourselves, we can come up with a pretty long list. Take just a moment here to reflect on your various temptations or trials past and present. Have you made any progress over time? Are you beginning to conquer some? Are you doing these battles with the help of the Holy Spirit?

Does Romans 12:1&2 give you encouragement, or does it?

What does it mean to be a living sacrifice?

How does one "Renew" their mind? (2 Cor 10:4&5)

How do we take captive our thoughts?

I, Stephen, have struggled for years with one particular temptation. I felt that this one stronghold wouldn't get broken. I first had to humble myself in the small group that I attended so that I had accountability and then I daily spent time in God's Word seeking a deeper relationship. One day I realized that my trial had gone away. When I skip my devotional time I notice the temptation beginning to get a foothold.

※♥ℰℭℛℰℭℛℰℭ♥℘

TUESDAY

※♥ℰℭℛℰℭℛℰℭ♥℘

Has your Christian experience been a contact sport? Have you been out in the practice fields developing your technique?

It would be difficult to read the New Testament and not pick up on the sport theme or the military theme of practice and training one's body. Paul must have spent time going to some local sporting events and noticed how disciplined these athletes were. It didn't take him long to figure out that these were good illustration for how we were to be in our spiritual practices as well.

Do a word search for discipline, armor, battle, practice, running the race, goal and other words that you would think of in this area and see what you get.

Are you being encouraged by your church to participate in some of these activities?

What would these look like to you, would you recognize it when presented?

The church at one point was the center of spiritual activity. Now, the movement is for small groups to get together at homes, restaurants, bars, tattoo parlors or other comfortable places where common everyday people can talk about those things that are important to God.

Let us continue to look at knowing God's will and knowing what the right path is so that we are not tempted to go away from God, but towards God. Turn to 1 John 4:1-6 and read carefully the text.

In our generation where do we get our information from?

Have we asked the hard questions of informational sources? What world view do they have? Does their world view line up with the scriptures?

How would we know if the information we listen to on the radio, television, books, newspapers, blogs, twitter, movies, friends, or co-workers is part of God's plan? The first verse says that we are to test the spirits to know if they are from God. It is critical to fully understand this point to know that we live in a world that is truly spirit led. We battle against the forces of good and evil every day. What lies behind the information given to us? Who is truly trying to give the message?

Verse four holds a key to the truth about this matter. We have the Spirit of the living God within those who have accepted the calling of the Holy Spirit. We have come alongside of God and are now willing to let God lead our lives. When we do this the Spirit inside of us guides each of us through the daily grind.

125

THURSDAY

The last chapter talked about living in the world and the world would rub off onto our clothing. This chapter continues that theme with being tempted to participate in the world's actions. When we enter through the family entrance we come to the mudroom where we can sit down and take the time to examine ourselves. This is where we allow the mirror of scripture to speak to us. It is by daily getting into God's word that we will even know that we have become unclean.

Scripture in conjunction with the Holy Spirit gives us the opportunity, if we allow it, to examine ourselves to find the areas that need to be washed again.

Paul in 1 Corinthians 11:27-32 is talking to those who are living in Corinth about how to have proper love for each other and to live in peace with their Savior. Paul is letting them know that they are weak in their faith because they do not set aside the time for self-examination.

Take time each day to pray that God will show you the areas that you need to wash up. So, up until now have you missed a spot here and there?

When God has revealed an issue in your life have you been willing to let go of it and to let God take control of those areas?

FRIDAY

Here's the challenge for you.

Find a significant way that you could get involved at your church.

If you don't have a church don't just join in somewhere or anywhere. Church is no longer just a Sunday event. Look for a church that first allows the truth of God's Word to be revealed. This may take some time to realize. Don't be shy; ask.

If you can't find a church home that has small group meetings, don't wait for them to meet your needs. Decide on your own to start a support group in your home or at a restaurant. Get involved. Become a leader.

Become a participant. Get involved. The real church happens outside of the bookends, it happens Monday through Saturday where we live our lives.

If you are truly unable to find a place to call home Stephen would love to have you visit the KonXions.org website. Here you will find information on how to get more involved in small KonXional small groups.

CHAPTER SEVEN

YOURS TRULY,
SERVANT OF GOD

"For thine is the kingdom, and the power,
and the glory forever. Amen"

Our country was built on lonely riders crossing the Great Plains, forging across flooded rivers, becoming snowbound in the great mountain ranges so our ancestors could read news about what was going on at home. Men, seeking their fortunes, were cold and tired from working the streams that were reluctant in giving up their treasures, would lie awake at night reading and rereading letters from their wives and children.

We at one time cherished the art of letter writing. We would communicate all that was in our hearts and bare our souls. Now, we don't have to wait days or weeks to receive important information. Now we pick up the phone, send a fax, tweet or facebook, or for those with a smart phone; email or instant message.

129

When you read those letters all you had to do was to look to the signature line to see what type of relationship the writer had with the intended reader. For the most part, if friends were writing to each other, it may have been signed with a "Your Friend" or just their name. Business correspondence would have ended with "Sincerely," or in many cases I will end it with "Christ's Servant." But, love letters will have words like "Love," "Yours forever", or simply "Yours."

"For thine is the kingdom, and the power,
and the glory forever. Amen"

The Apostles ended The Lord's Prayer in a similar fashion to a love letter. They wanted to end the same way that it started. They wanted to focus on the fact that it was God who was in control and should receive their worship and praise.

The Apostles have been credited with adding the last line to the Lord's Prayer. Some will argue that it is found in the King James Version; so therefore, Christ must have said it. Later translations, like the NIV, have gone back to the original texts and have found no trace of this line.

Regardless of how it ends, our mission is to apply this prayer to our daily life. If Jesus took the time to give this as an example to his followers, then two thousand years later we still should follow his example. This prayer cannot and will not go out of style. How then, can we apply it today to our lives?

Well, that is the mission for us today. I will give you an example of what it could sound like, and then, your assignment is to create some prayers on your own.

Practice Prayer:

Child going off to school for the first time.

Father, we put our daughter into your loving hands as she goes off to kindergarten. Father, be with all of the other students and the teachers that will make up this new environment for Joan. Let you name be remembered with honor while she is there.

Let your kingdom shine bright as Joan shows love and concern to those around her.

Give her the ability to learn more about your world and her place in it.

Help her to remember that she will need your help when she fails, and help her to be sensitive to others as they fall short of perfect. Help her to forgive those that may hurt her feelings.

Father, I pray that you will help her in the little tests, and prepare her for those big battles when the enemy wants to cut her down.

Father, you are God above all other gods. Help us, as parents to remember that you love her more than we do. We give you all of the respect that you deserve. Amen

Take each one of these statements and develop your prayer. Remember, these are to be real prayers for real people who live in a real world.

Child or a person we know going into the military....

How should we pray for our job and those we come in contact with....

How could we pray for the new day that we are going to start

How can we pray for the church we attend....

Saturday

(place your reflections on this page)

❧ ᏽᏽᏽᏽᏽᏽ ☙

Sunday

❧ ᏽᏽᏽᏽᏽᏽ ☙

(place your prayer or prayers here)

YOUR AUTHOR
STEPHEN CROWELL

For most of Stephen's childhood he lived on what was his grandparent's farm in Western New York. The forests were his playground. At the time he loved the winter months, building ice forts and skiing on the back hill. Now; though, Stephen has a hard time with the winter's cold and snow after living all over the southern states of America.

Stephen was fortunate to have served as youth and young adult pastor under his father in two different Wesleyan Churches. He then was asked to serve a small rural church in Leon, New York with is famous for their Amish community (hence the reference in the book). While serving as a pastor, Stephen completed his Outdoor-Recreation degree from Houghton College. This degree came in handy when Stephen served as a camp director for the United Methodist Church in Pennsylvania.

Currently Stephen is serving as a senior pastor back in Western New York for the United Methodist Church. His passion has been working to develop an emerging church model. Stephen desires to bring people back to the radical message that Jesus taught his disciples. We have a responsibility to be in close intimate fellowship groups that help to support each other through the good and the bad.

Jesus also taught us to have an outward looking focus. Stephen understands that the message of the cross is for those who are marginalized and are sitting on the fringes. He believes that we need to break down all barriers to the foot of the cross. Another area that Stephen feels is important for the community of Christ's followers is to come together regularly to share common meals. It seems that scripture is regularly depicting Jesus eating with friends, relatives, strangers, and most importantly sinners.

Stephen is dedicated to spending any and all spare time traveling with his wife, Kristan, and with any of the kids that desire to come along. They have eight children, one of which is a daughter-in-law. They now use the excuse that the kids live in different parts of the country to visit with them. (Texas, Alaska, Florida)

If this book has helped you with your life's journey Stephen would love to hear from you. If you have a story about how this prayer has helped you, or changed your life, please share it with him @ pastor@konxions.org.

May God bless you on your journey.
Pastor Stephen Crowell

Made in the USA
Charleston, SC
24 October 2011